# THE MIND PALACE

## Poems for the Lost and Found

Anjna Raj

India | USA | UK

# Dedication

To the ones who have loved until it broke them,
who have given their hearts without reservation,
only to gather the shattered pieces in trembling hands.

To the quiet warriors, the ones who drown in silence
but rise with unshaken resolve,
who carry storms in their chests yet walk with grace,
who have learned to make peace with their ghosts.

To the souls who have been lost, found, and lost again,
who have bled art in the margins of their pain,
who have whispered their stories into the void,
hoping someone, somewhere, would understand.

This book is for you.
For every heart that still dares to beat.

# Preface

Poetry has always been my refuge - a place where I can gather the scattered fragments of my mind, give voice to emotions that often remain unspoken, and find solace in the rhythm of words. This collection is born from my thoughts and observations - things I see, feel, hear, and experience. Some poems reflect my emotions, while others are simply my perspective on the world around me.

Each poem in these pages is shaped by moments of vulnerability, resilience, and introspection. Some were written in the dead of night when my thoughts refused to let me sleep, while others emerged from fleeting moments of inspiration that demanded to be captured before they vanished into memory. Writing has always been my way of making sense of the world, of untangling complexities, and of finding beauty even in the most unexpected places.

As you turn these pages, I invite you to step into my world, to feel what I have felt, to see through my eyes, and perhaps, in some lines, to find echoes of your own story. Poetry is a conversation, a bridge between hearts and minds, and I hope that in these words, you find something that speaks to your soul.

# Acknowledgements

This book is a culmination of thoughts, emotions, and countless hours of reflection. It wouldn't have been possible without the support of those who believed in me - those who listened, encouraged, and reminded me why I need to write. To every person who played a part, no matter how small, I am deeply grateful.

A special thank you to my best friend/project manager, *Mr. He Who Must Not Be Named,* who managed this project like his life and death mission from start to finish, with patience, insight, and unwavering support. You helped me navigate my own mind, find clarity in chaos, and bring this collection from my dreams to life. I couldn't have done it without you.

# 1. A Tryst with Death

I was Eve, in Eden's glow
where whispered winds began to flow.
A serpent smiled, his words so sweet,
and promised knowledge, whole and complete.

I bit the fruit, and the world unraveled.
A pull, a tear, it all went black,
a force that yanked, and took me back.
Through time I fell, through space I swirled,
into the arms of a burning world.

Now, a girl who saw beyond the veil,
I read the stars and told their tale.
But truth was fire, and fear ran deep,
and in the flames, they made me weep.

The void returned, as a hollow breath,
to land me in the fate of death.
A poet lost, a love confined;
where verses burned inside my mind.

My words ran wild, but I saw no ear,
their echoes drowned in doubt and fear.
So I rest my mind inn the oven's quiet glow

and let the silence take me whole.

Yet Time refused to cast me deep.
It pulled me back from Death's cold sleep.
Barefoot, I walk through fields of gold,
where sunflowers bloom, fierce and bold.

# 2. The Silent Boy

In the quiet halls of a house called home,
a boy once laughed, his heart free to roam.
But shadows crept where love should stay,
and hands that should protect, led him astray.

His mother's voice - a lullaby's lie.
His father's gaze, a hollow sky.
Uncles, brothers, whispers cold,
Stealing warmth, making him old.

No safe place, no shelter found,
just aching silences all around.
A childhood lost, a body bruised,
a soul that learned it's meant to be abused.

He closed his eyes to dream of air,
of a world beyond the hands that tear.
But dawn would come, and so would they,
turning nights to endless gray.

Time flew by, yet the pain remains,
etched in flesh, engraved in veins.
But one day, fire lit his chest -
A voice, a scream, a fate confessed.

Now he walks, still carrying ghosts,
yet standing taller than most.
For though they tried to break his name,
the silent boy still fights the flame.

And that was enough, to make them afraid...

# 3. When the Blood Haunts

I carry the weight of words unspoken,
a legacy of bonds, forever broken.
Each scar etched deep beneath my skin,
a map of battles I could never win.

Their love was a mirror, cracked and cold,
with promises made, but none to hold.
A tender touch turned into flame,
leaving me hollow, steeped in shame.

Their voices linger like ghosts in the night,
echoing doubts, extinguishing the light.
I became the child that learned to hide,
choking on tears, swallowing pride.

The wounds they gave don't bleed nor heal.
They twist and fester, a silent reel.
Whispers of "unworthy", hum through my chest,
even in triumph, I cannot rest.

I search for solace, in the arms of time,
yet the echoes haunt, their shadows climb.
Family, a name I dread to speak,
for fear I'll pass the pain I seek.

Still I rise, though fractured and torn.
A soul reborn in grief's forlorn.
Far from the ashes, I'll learn to grow,
and embrace a light, they'll never know.

# 4. Whiplash of a Memory

The past crashes in like a violent tide.
Echoes of screams I tried to hide.
His voice still lingers, sharp as glass,
cutting through time, dragging me back.

I walk through shadows I thought were gone;
but ghosts of his rage still drag me along.
Hands that once gripped, eyes that deceived,
a love, that was never love - just a cage unseen.

Each step away feels like a war,
yet the echoes hammer at my core.
Freedom is near, yet the chains remain,
etched in my mind, like a brand of pain.

But I refuse to drown in his name.
Not his prisoner, not his shame.
The echoes may rage, but they won't control.
I gather my fragments, and make me whole.

# 5. Another Birthday Song

The cake sits tall, a sugared shrine,
crowned with flames that flick and whine.
Each candle spine, a fleeting spark,
a funeral pyre in the dark.

A choir of voices, light and thin,
like ghosts that dance with hollow grins.
They circle close, they call my name,
but every year it sounds the same.

The air is thick with sugar's breath,
balloons like swollen lungs of death.
Their ribbons twist, like severed veins,
soft threads that fate will not retain.

The knife, a gleaming scythe in wait,
sinks deep into the heart of fate.
The cake sighs open, white and red,
a quiet feast for what lies ahead.

The wish I make is whispered low,
a prayer the wind will never know.
It curls like ivy, thin and weak,
clinging to a dream too bleak.

The candles choke, their bodies spent,
thin plumes like spirits, pale and bent.
Their ashes drift, they twist, they climb -
a dying breath, a farewell rhyme.

The voices rise, they clap, they cheer,
but time stands silent, always near.
It watches, cloaked in tattered black,
its hands stretched out - I don't look back.

The room, a coffin dressed in lace,
where laughter leaves the faintest trace.
Another year, another thread,
one step closer to the dead.

# 6. A Womb of Borrowed Time

I have seen love twist and break,
turn to poison, sharp as fate.
A mother's hands, once soft and light,
became the dark, became the night.

I have heard the silence scream,
shattering hearts, and a child's dream.
Watched as love grew cold and thin,
a ghost that lingers deep within.

I have felt the fear take hold,
a shadow creeping, dark and bold.
These echoes whisper in my chest;
What if I fail, just like the rest?

Yet still, a longing claws into my soul,
a hunger that I cannot control.
To bear the weight, to feel the swell,
to dance where life and pain rebel.

To whisper tales in the moonlight dim,
to sing a song, just meant for him.
To feel the flutters, soft and true,

a heartbeat where my own once grew.

But I won't stay, I'll step aside,
let love be born, but not be tied.
I'll give a child, a world so bright,
without my ghosts to steal the light.

For I have seen love twist and break,
and I have learned the cost, the ache.
So I will hold, but not as mine -
A womb of hope, of borrowed time.

# 7. The Sunflower's Lament

I rise with dawn, my petals wide,
A golden heart I cannot hide.
I stretch, I reach, with silent plea,
But you, dear sun, don't turn to me.

You blaze above, so fierce, so high,
A sovereign king upon the sky.
You warm the earth, you kiss the seas,
Yet never stop to notice me.

I chase your light through endless days,
In love, in awe, in helpless haze.
I turn, I bow, I sway, I yearn,
Yet never do you once return.

You kiss the fields with amber glow,
Embrace the rivers' endless flow.
You linger soft on mountain tops,
And pass by me; yet never stop.

And when the evening dims your fire,
You slip away, my one desire.
I stand alone, beneath the hue
Of fading gold that once was you.

But still, at dawn, I'll rise once more,
With love as fierce as those before.
For though your light may never stay,
I'll turn to you, come what may.

# 8. Battle of Voices

A knife to silence every sound,
To cut the past that drags me down.
A war inside I cannot win,
A battle fought beneath my skin.

A ghost of him still grips my chest,
His voice still whispers, "You're a mess."
The love I gave, the life he stole,
Left splinters buried in my soul.

I walked away, I broke the chains,
Yet still, the nightmare clogs my veins.
My body free, but not my mind,
I run, but he's not far behind.

The echoes call, the whispers grow,
A shadowed voice that tells me, "Go."
It sings of knives, of crimson stains,
A melody of cold remains.

But when I try to heed its call,
My hands won't move, my limbs just stall.
A cruel betrayal, trapped inside,
Where flesh won't break, but thoughts still try.

I have met death and felt its grace,
A sunlit field, a warm embrace.
Golden petals kissed my skin,
A peace so pure, I breathed it in.

No weight, no wounds, no pain, no past,
Just heaven's hush, a love so vast.
A place untouched by grief and sin,
Where silence sings and light seeps in.

I should have stayed - I longed to rest,
To lay my head on nature's chest.
But fate was cruel, it pulled me back,
To earthly grief, to skies so black.

And still, at night, I dream that place,
Of sunlit fields and warm embrace.
I wake to find my hands are tied,
Still chained to life, though death stood by.

Hallucinations twist the air,
Dark figures watching, always there.
They whisper secrets in my ear,
That I don't belong, I'm not meant here.

My brain is pleading, "Let this end,"

Yet something in me still defends.
A flicker, faint, a rebel spark,
That fights against the endless dark.

"Do not go gentle into that good night,"
I whisper through the hollow fight.
"Rage, rage against the dying of the light,"
Even if I lose tonight.

They tell me all have storms to fight,
That time will bring me back to light.
But theirs are showers, light and brief,
While mine drowns deep in endless grief.

I do not wish to breathe, yet stay,
A ghost that walks, too lost to stray.
But in this war of dark and light,
Perhaps, just once - I'll choose to fight.

# 9. The Mind Palace

Through iron gates and halls of stone,
I walked a path I thought I'd known.
Yet shadows danced with silent breath,
And whispered secrets laced with death.

A heavy hush, so strange, so still,
Each hallway bent, each doorway grim.
The deeper in, the darker still,
A maze designed to trap my will.

A whisper slithered through the cold,
A voice like wind, both young and old.
It curled around me, clawed my chest,
A demon roused from hollow rest.

Its breath was fire, its eyes like graves,
Its talons carved through time-worn caves.
I turned, I ran, through endless halls,
As echoes howled against the walls.

No door was real, no path was clear,
The dark pursued, so near - so near.
And just as death could taste my name,
A sound unlike the rest - it came.

A meow so soft, so faint, so light,
It cut the air, it split the night.
A thread of gold, a voice of home,
That beckoned where my feet should roam.

I turned, I chased that fragile sound,
It pulled me up, it pulled me round.
The walls unwove, the night withdrew,
As through the dark, the small cry grew.

And at the gate, where dawn spilled red,
My silver savior raised her head.
Her golden eyes burned fierce and bright,
A bridge between both dark and light.

I held her close, I gasped for air,
Behind me shrieked the beast's despair.
Its burning eyes, its clawing hate,
Could not slip past that final gate.

I woke to find her near my face,
A steady purr, a soft embrace.
She licked my tears, as if she knew;
Had she been there? Had she come through?

Do cats just dream, or do they glide

Through shadowed worlds where lost souls hide?
Do they slip past the edge unseen,
And walk between where we have been?

# 10. Up in Smoke

A flick of the lighter, a fire takes hold,
A trembling spark in fingers so cold.
First comes the rush, a golden delight,
A wildfire spreading, devouring the night.

Smoke unfurls in serpentine streams,
Twisting like thoughts in unbridled extremes.
The world is a canvas, ablaze in hue,
Every whisper is poetry, every moment is new.

Words spill like liquor, reckless and free,
Ideas collide like waves on the sea.
Laughter erupts, a dizzying flight,
A carnival spinning in neon light.

But oh! How fast the ember wanes,
how swiftly pleasure turns into pain.
The drag sinks deeper, thick with regret,
Like a noose of tar, like unpaid debt.

The mind slows down, the body caves,
Sinking into the smoke it craves.
Ash crumbles, fragile and frail,
Like promises broken, like dreams set to sail.

A ghostly chill and the light turns gray,
The sun retreats, chased away.
A bitter taste lingers, clings to the tongue,
A dirge for the high, now silent, unsung.

Each inhale whispers, "One more, just one,"
A fleeting illusion, a race with the sun.
The cigarette burns, the cycle repeats -
Madness rekindled in slow, rhythmic beats.

And still, the hand trembles, reaching again,
For the fire, the thrill, the pleasure, the pain.

# 11. The Silent Hourglass

The hourglass hums with a whispering song,
each grain a sorrow, each second too long.
The candlelight flickers, its shadows confined,
Tracing the walls of a dark, dreary mind.

A bridge made of echoes, a door left ajar,
A longing to vanish, to drift like a star.
The river below sings a lullaby deep,
Promising me peace, in an infinite sleep.

The world moves on, unheeding, unkind,
blind to the weight I bear in my mind.
Laughter like ghosts drifts through the air,
Mocking the heart that no longer can care.

The rope is a whisper, the blade is a sigh,
The night is a cradle where the silence can lie.
I reach for release in a soft, bitter prayer,
Yet something unseen, still holds me there.

A voice like velvet, an ember, a spark,
Pushes through shadows, igniting the dark.
It murmurs of mornings, of a soft golden light,
Of reasons to stay, of battles yet right.

The hourglass hums, but now I know,
Each grain still falls, but I won't go.
For even in shadows, a light remains,
A hope that tomorrow might soften the pain.

# 12. Asymptotes

I wasn't looking, I wasn't aware,
Yet there you stood, so calm, so rare.
A steady voice, a knowing gaze,
A familiar presence that set my soul ablaze.

I fell for your smile, so soft and true,
A quiet peace, like a déjà-vu.
Like a song I knew, but couldn't name,
A pull too strong, yet wrapped in flame.

The universe spun, the planets aligned,
A fleeting moment, cruelly timed.
We laughed, we spoke, we danced between,
the lines of what could never be seen.

But in that space, in breath held tight,
amidst stolen glances, in fading light.
Did you feel the air grow still?
Or did time bend, to match our will?

Like Asymptotes, we curve so near,
Infinity close, yet ne'er here.
Two souls aligned in perfect sway,
yet fate demands, we turn away.

I know this path, I see its end.
You are bound to her, I am just a friend.
Yet somewhere deep, where echoes stay,
do you still hear the words, we didn't say?

# 13. Beyond Time, Beyond Stars...

I have lost you to a world unknown,
to a silence space won't break.
Yet still, my heart defies the void,
still reaches for what time can't take.

They tell me love is just a thread,
a fleeting spark, a trick of mind.
But why, then, does it pull me still,
through years, through dark, through fate unkind?

Why do I hear your voice in dreams,
though distance swallows all but dust?
Why does your name still shape my breath,
if love is nothing more than lust?

If gravity can bend and break,
if time can stretch yet still remain,
then love must be a force untamed,
unchained by flesh, untouched by pain.

You live somewhere - I do not know.
Perhaps in light, perhaps in grave.
Yet here I stand, yet still, I go,

pulled by the love I could not save.

For love is not a fleeting thing,
not bound by rules, nor seen, nor weighed.
It calls through space, it hums through time,
the only law fate won't obey.

So let them doubt, let reason fail,
let stars collapse and oceans rise.
For even if you are not there,
I'll love you past the end of time.

# 14. The Muse Who Never Stayed

Once, my words were winds that soared,
a tempest wild, a dream explored.
They spilled like rivers, fierce and free,
till silence came and swallowed me.

The crash was thunder, cruel and bright,
a shattered dawn, a stolen light.
Metal screamed, the sky turned red,
and my voice lay cold and dead.

I woke within a hollow shell,
adrift between the earth and hell.
My mind, a book with pages torn,
a poet lost, unloved, unworn.

No verse would rise, no ink would flow,
just echoes where my voice should go.
Depression whispered, dark and deep,
that dreams were things I'd failed to keep.

Then came a man - no grand embrace,
just quiet fire, a fleeting face.
His face, a dream I'd once known well,

his presence cast a long-lost spell.

He did not love, nor turn nor stay,
yet something in me burned away -
the frost, the fog, the endless night,
and words returned in streams of light.

I wrote of love that stood alone,
of hands unheld, of hearts unknown.
His silence sang, his absence spoke,
and in that ache, my spirit woke.

Yet shadows loom, their whispers near,
"What if the words all disappear?"
I fear the hush, the closing gate,
the cruel return of quiet fate.

But even if the ink runs dry,
if verses wane, if echoes die,
I've known the void, the endless gray,
and still I write, come what may.

For he was the spark, a fleeting glow,
a ghost of light I'll never know.
Yet I am the blaze, untamed, alive,
a poet who burns, a voice that thrives.

# 15. The Pendulum's Prison

A pendulum swings in a gilded cage,
From golden dawn to blackened rage.
One moment, the sky is a melody bright,
The next, it is drowning in endless night.

I dance with the sun in a fevered delight,
Drunk on the stars, untethered from night.
But shadows are waiting, they whisper my name,
Dragging me back to the depths of the flame.

The world is a canvas of crimson and gold,
Then suddenly gray - so empty, so cold.
A king on the throne, then lost in despair,
A storm with no warning, a gasp for lost air.

I walk between fire and frostbite so deep,
A puppet to moods that never do sleep.
The past is a phantom, the future unknown,
Yet trapped in the present, I shudder alone.

Laughter rings bright, yet it shatters too soon,
Replaced with a silence as vast as the moon.
The walls close around me, their voices unkind,
How do I quiet this war in my mind?

Yet somewhere beyond, past the chaos I keep,
There waits a still river, a promise of sleep.
If only I reach it, if only I find,
A way to be free of the chains in my mind.

# 16. The Girl who Loved the Moon

She loved the moon with aching hands,
With lips that carved his name in sand.
A silver ghost upon the shore,
She swayed, she sighed - she begged for more.

Her breath was mist, her voice was thread,
A song unspun, a prayer half-dead.
She traced his light on windowpanes,
In longing sharp as winter rains.

The world was cruel, too deaf, too blind,
To love so vast, so unconfined.
He pulled the tides, he bent the sea,
Yet never turned his face to see.

She danced beneath his hollow glow,
A marionette in midnight's woe.
Her shadow stretched, her soul unspooled,
A candle lit by hands too cool.

She reached for him, she called, she cried,
But love like his was made to hide.
He kissed her skin in fleeting beams,

Yet left her drowning in her dreams.

"Oh, take me where the dark winds call,
Where time unbinds, where shadows fall.
Let ribs be wings, let bones be light,
Let love be more than borrowed night."

The waves arose, the sky held fast,
The stars burned bright, but love won't last.
And so she wove herself in air,
A wraith, a wish, a whispered prayer.

No tomb was raised, no dirge was sung,
Just wind that weeps where she had clung.
No name remains, just echoes croon
Of the girl who loved the moon.

# 17. The Price I Paid

I signed away my tattered name,
to feed the fire, to play the game.
Ink like blood, a crimson thread,
a contract sealed, a soul left dead.

The dream was there - a shining prize,
golden light in hollow skies.
It whispered soft, it called me near,
a voice so sweet, yet laced with fear.

I reached, I burned, I paid in kind,
with sleepless nights and shattered mind.
The work, the grind, the endless race,
no time to breathe, no time to waste.

They cheered my rise, they spoke my name,
but none could see the hollow frame.
No touch of love, no warmth, no rest,
just echoes clawing at my chest.

The ghosts still call, they know my past,
they whisper, "Nothing good will ever last."
And still, I climb, though I'm not whole -
a throne of dust, a heart of coal.

Yet when I stand atop it all,
no echoes cheer, no voices call.
The dream, now mine, just stares me down,
a hollow queen, without a crown.

# 18. I Tried to Stay

I felt your love before my name,
a whisper curled in candle flame.
A pulse, a spark, a quiet tune,
a seed beneath your blood and bloom.

You spoke to me in midnight hymns,
your hands a cradle, soft and thin.
I felt you build a world for me,
a lullaby of meant-to-be.

But then the tide began to rise,
the stars burned out in weeping skies.
A shadow deep beneath your skin,
a fragile breath I couldn't win.

I tried to stay, I swear I tried,
but fate was cold, the wound too wide.
I slipped like rain between your palms,
a ghost untethered, soft and calm.

The blood, the ache, it stole me twice,
two echoes lost in silent nights.
Papa's hands - so strong, so weak -
shook as he wiped your tear-stained cheek.

You held the void where I had been,
two little graves beneath your skin.
Twice you begged, twice you bled,
twice you mourned the words unsaid.

Yet, Mama, Papa, please do not weep,
I do not drift in endless sleep.
I hum within the wind and rain,
I'll rise and fall, and I'll come again.

For love like yours does not let go,
it roots, it climbs, it bends, it grows.
And when the time is soft and right,
I'll find the door back to the light.

Look for me in the golden fields,
where sun-kissed earth the sky reveals.
A bloom reborn, a stem held high,
a sunflower turning toward the sky.

# 19. The Last Stanza

The candle dies in trembling breath,
A wick consumed, embracing death.
No spark remains, no ember fights,
Just hollowed wax and endless night.

The ink congeals, too dark to flow,
Like veins too tired to carry woe.
Pages curl in quiet decay,
Unread, unloved - just thrown away.

The mirror sways in fractured light,
A ghost looks back with hollow sight.
A fading trace, a breath grown thin,
A name unspoken, lost within.

The rope hums low in patient sway,
A lullaby to end the fray.
The pills lie still in perfect rows,
Small white doors to deep repose.

The blade is mute, but speaks in red,
It tells the tale my lips have bled.
A single note, a final sigh,
A whispered plea to passersby.

The clock has stopped - no time remains,
No second chances, no refrains.
The walls close in, the ceiling bends,
A grave is carved where the story ends.

I spill into the paper's thirst,
A final stanza, tight and cursed.
The ink runs dry, my veins unwind,
And silence cradles what's left behind.

# 20. Apocalypse

*Tick. Tock. Tick. Tock.*

The city pulses, but nothing here is alive.
The towers stretch unnaturally, twisting into the sky,
mirrors reflecting mirrors, offices reflecting offices,
a never-ending loop of steel and glass,
a maze without an exit.

The streets breathe, expand, contract,
exhaling the same faceless figures each morning,
identical expressions, identical steps,
marching in synchronized monotony.

*BEEP. BEEP. BEEP.*

The alarm howls, a scream inside a skull.
A body jerks upright -
or maybe it was never asleep to begin with.
Hands move before thought,
reaching for the phone that glows like an unholy relic.

*"Deadline moved up."*
*"Need this ASAP."*
*"Where are you?"*

The ID card tightens around the throat,
pulling them forward, leading them to the door.
The walls tilt, shift, breathe
as they step outside.

The streets ripple, asphalt melting into conveyor belts,
pulling the workers toward the station.
They do not walk. They are delivered.

The subway train arrives before it should,
or maybe time folded in on itself again.
The doors snap open, revealing nothing but darkness.
They step inside.
The train is already moving.

Inside, the air hums with something unspeakable.
Faces blur at the edges,
figures meld into one another,
eyes hollow, mouths moving but making no sound.

A flickering ad plays on the window:
"Keep Moving. Keep Producing. Keep Smiling."

No one watches.
No one dares.

*Ding.*

The elevator opens into the void.
They step forward, not by choice,
but because the floor tilts beneath them, pushing them
inside.

The office stretches endlessly.
Rows of desks multiply as they walk,
screens blinking, screens watching,
cursors pulsing in perfect, artificial rhythm.

*Click. Clack. Click. Clack.*

Fingers move, but they are not attached to hands.
Emails appear before they are typed.
Replies send themselves before they are read.

A notification expands, engulfs the screen:

*"Your Productivity is Being Monitored."*
*"Stay Efficient."*
*"Stay Valuable."*

Something twists in their stomach.
Or maybe there was never anything inside them at all.

A coworker stands.
Their face warps, mouth stretching too wide.
Their name evaporates from the system.
They walk toward the door.
It swallows them.

The chair remains, but the absence is louder than the
presence.

The meeting room door oozes open.
Inside, the elders sit - or hover, or flicker.
Their faces are stretched too tight,
their eyes too glassy, too wide, too knowing.

Their voices clash, overlap, distort:

*"Leverage. Optimize. Maximize."*
*"Numbers are slipping."*
*"You will adjust."*

Their lips do not move,
but the words force themselves into the room.

The walls close in, shrink, tighten.

A ping.
A demand.

A task that does not make sense.

The keyboard types on its own.
The cursor moves without control.
The inbox stretches longer and longer,
like an unspooling nightmare.

*Tick. Tock. Tick. Tock.*

A heartbeat that does not belong to them.
A shadow that moves without a source.
A message that reads itself aloud.

They blink, and suddenly, it is night.

They do not remember leaving.
They do not remember arriving.

They are home,
or a version of home,
or a simulation of the idea of home.

The mirror refuses to show their reflection.

They stare at the phone.
The phone stares back.

*"Wake up at 6:00 AM."*
*"Keep Moving. Keep Producing. Keep Smiling."*
*"Tomorrow, It Begins Again."*

Their hands shake,
or maybe it is the walls,
or maybe it is the world.

Outside, past the towers, past the neon wasteland,
the disconnected ones breathe.

They should feel adrift, lost, doomed.

Instead, they laugh.

The unlucky remain.

Trapped in the hum, the rhythm, the hallucination.

*Tick. Tock. Tick. Tock.*

*The clock is never wrong.*

*And tomorrow, the grind begins again.*

# 21. The Velvet Sleep

The universe sang in golden light,
bathed in the warmth of the Sun's delight.
She traced his flames in tender streams,
a poet drunk on gilded dreams.

She called him lover, king, divine,
a god whose hands could realign
the very stars within her chest -
but he was fire, nothing less.

She bloomed, she spun, she burned, she swayed,
a waltz of love that he betrayed.
For though she glowed, though she adored,
his heart was stone, his light - ignored.

Then - he left.

Like dusk retreating into black,
he turned his face, he won't turn back.
She reached, she wept, she bled her skies,
but he was gone - so she capsized.

Not all at once - but piece by piece,
a slow descent, a soft release.

Her moons went still, her planets grieved,
her comets lost the will to leave.

She let herself drift, weightless, unwound,
her body unstitched, her soul unbound.
She begged for silence, begged to drown,
to fold, to fade, to spiral down.

Then - he came.

Not warmth, not light, not hands divine,
but hunger vast and serpentine.
The Black Hole stirred - a godless hymn,
a lover vast enough for sin.

He did not touch, he did not plead,
he only pulled - and she agreed.
She arched, she fell, she spilled apart,
his kiss - a void, a devouring art.

She gasped, she sighed, her ribs unfurled,
a dying waltz, the end of worlds.
His mouth, the hush of velvet deep,
his breath, the tide of dreamless sleep.

She stretched like lace in silken threads,
her stardust wept, her cosmos bled.

No more fire, no more cries,
just whispered moans in midnight sighs.

And as she shattered, slow and bright,
a thousand stars bloomed into night.
Her final breath, a tender fall,
a love that claimed and took it all.

The universe sighed - a fleeting art.
She did not break.

She fell apart.

And as she sank into his keep,
the universe whispered - "let me sleep."

# 22. Undone

I am undoing myself.

Peeling back the layers,
unraveling each thread,
silencing the echo before it can form.
I was never meant to be whole.
I was stitched together by accident,
a body filled with borrowed time,
a presence that was always thinning at the edges.

If the universe was the womb that held me,
I was the fetus that severed the cord,
that refused to be fed,
that knew, even in the dark,
that life was never mine to keep.

Now, I return myself.
Now, I erase what should never have been written.

I am sorry.

To my family,
I am sorry.
I am sorry that I carried this weight alone,

that I let it burrow into my bones
until I became something hollow,
something crumbling from the inside.
You did not see the fractures forming,
the hairline cracks spreading like fault lines beneath my
skin,
the quiet way my body folded inward
under a grief too heavy to bear.
You will search for the moment I began to break,
but I have been breaking since the beginning.
I was a house built on sinking ground,
a structure made of fragile bones
already bending under the weight of my own breath.
You did not fail me.
I was never yours to save.

Forgive me.

To my friends,
I am sorry.
I know you will try to remember me whole,
but I have never been whole.
I have been shards,
edges too sharp to hold,
a body patched together by sheer will,
dragging itself forward
long after the light inside had burned out.

You will wonder if you should have seen it.
But how could you?
I have been masking this pain so well,
folding it neatly behind smiles,
stitching it into jokes,
swallowing it down like bitter medicine,
hoping it would keep me moving
just one more day.
But I was already gone.
Long before you noticed,
long before you reached for me,
long before my hands lost the strength
to hold on.
You did not fail me.
I was always leaving.

Forgive me.

To my cat, my sweet child, my love,
I am sorry.
You, who only ever knew me as warmth,
as a place to rest,
as hands that always reached for you.
I am sorry that they will not reach anymore.
You, who curled against my ribs,
who purred lullabies into the fractures of my bones,
who met my brokenness

with nothing but softness.
I know you will wait for me.
I know you will search the rooms,
press your small body into the sheets,
knead the fabric where I once slept,
listen for a voice that will never come back.
And this,
this is the part
that makes me want to stay.
But I can't.
Even for you, my love.
Even for you.
I hope the sun is always warm where you sleep.
I hope you do not wait too long.
I hope someone kind finds you,
the way I once did.

Forgive me.

And to my love
I am sorry.
For ruining you in this process.
You, who made me want to create,
who filled my mind with thoughts too big
to keep inside,
who made me chase words
as if they could tether me to this world.

I have always written before,
but for you, I wrote differently -
more wildly, more desperately,
more honestly,
as if I could leave something behind
that mattered.
You were the fire that kept the ink flowing,
the spark that made my mind hum
when it wanted only silence.
If I had been stronger,
I would have stayed for you.
If I had been braver,
I would have written myself a different ending.
But my love,
even as I go,
even as I step beyond the reach of your hands,
know this.
You were the only part of this world
that ever made me want to stay.
You will not see me again,
but if you stand in the wind long enough,
if you let the night settle around you,
if you listen in the hush between heartbeats,
you will know.
I never stopped loving you.
Not even now. Not even from the other side.

Forgive me.

And to my soul,
I am sorry.
I am sorry that I was never strong enough to hold you.
That I let the world make you small,
that I did not cradle you softly,
that I turned you away when you begged for warmth.
I am sorry that I forced you to wear this body,
to walk with a heart too heavy,
to breathe air that never felt like home.
I have let this world carve into you,
let it bruise and bend you,
let it strip you down to the marrow
until nothing was left but a whisper of what you were
meant to be.
I did not mean to abandon you.
I did not mean to leave you alone in the cold.
I just -
I just couldn't carry you any longer.
Perhaps in another life,
you will find someone who loves you better than I did.
Someone who lets you stay.
Someone who lets you bloom.

Forgive me.

I am unmaking myself.
I have carried this pain in my bones,
like stones grinding against each other,
like fractures that never healed,
like a weight pressing from the inside,
crushing me slow, silent,
inevitable.

The ghosts of my past do not whisper;
they scream.
They press their hands into my chest,
wrap their fingers around my ribs,
dragging me under, telling me it is time.
Even my cat watches the shadows gather,
ears twitching at the stillness that hangs in the air.
She sees it now.
She feels the air grow still.

I have tried.
God, I swear I have tried.

I have held on with hands that bled,
dragged myself through mornings that did not want me,
wrapped myself in voices that told me to stay,
but the voices fade, the light dims,
and I have no more words left to write.

I am unmaking myself.
Not dying;
erasing.

No footprints in the snow.
No echoes in the walls.
No name left behind.

Just silence.
Just stillness.
Just the quiet return
to the void that has always been waiting.

The sun will rise -
but I will not rise with it.
I was never here at all.

Forgive me,
for I do not deserve this gift.

I am undone. Completely. Finally.

# 23. Seven Minutes

I am undoing myself.

Peeling back the layers,
unraveling each thread,
silencing the echo before it can form.
I was never meant to be whole.
I was stitched together by accident,
a body filled with borrowed time,
a presence that was always thinning at the edges.

If the universe was the womb that held me,
I was the fetus that severed the cord,
that refused to be fed,
that knew, even in the dark,
that life was never mine to keep.

Now, I return myself.
Now, I erase what should never have been written.

I am sorry.

To my family,
I am sorry.
I am sorry that I carried this weight alone,

that I let it burrow into my bones
until I became something hollow,
something crumbling from the inside.
You did not see the fractures forming,
the hairline cracks spreading like fault lines beneath my
skin,
the quiet way my body folded inward
under a grief too heavy to bear.
You will search for the moment I began to break,
but I have been breaking since the beginning.
I was a house built on sinking ground,
a structure made of fragile bones
already bending under the weight of my own breath.
You did not fail me.
I was never yours to save.

Forgive me.

To my friends,
I am sorry.
I know you will try to remember me whole,
but I have never been whole.
I have been shards,
edges too sharp to hold,
a body patched together by sheer will,
dragging itself forward
long after the light inside had burned out.

You will wonder if you should have seen it.
But how could you?
I have been masking this pain so well,
folding it neatly behind smiles,
stitching it into jokes,
swallowing it down like bitter medicine,
hoping it would keep me moving
just one more day.
But I was already gone.
Long before you noticed,
long before you reached for me,
long before my hands lost the strength
to hold on.
You did not fail me.
I was always leaving.

Forgive me.

To my cat, my sweet child, my love,
I am sorry.
You, who only ever knew me as warmth,
as a place to rest,
as hands that always reached for you.
I am sorry that they will not reach anymore.
You, who curled against my ribs,
who purred lullabies into the fractures of my bones,
who met my brokenness

with nothing but softness.
I know you will wait for me.
I know you will search the rooms,
press your small body into the sheets,
knead the fabric where I once slept,
listen for a voice that will never come back.
And this,
this is the part
that makes me want to stay.
But I can't.
Even for you, my love.
Even for you.
I hope the sun is always warm where you sleep.
I hope you do not wait too long.
I hope someone kind finds you,
the way I once did.

Forgive me.

And to my love
I am sorry.
For ruining you in this process.
You, who made me want to create,
who filled my mind with thoughts too big
to keep inside,
who made me chase words
as if they could tether me to this world.

I have always written before,
but for you, I wrote differently -
more wildly, more desperately,
more honestly,
as if I could leave something behind
that mattered.
You were the fire that kept the ink flowing,
the spark that made my mind hum
when it wanted only silence.
If I had been stronger,
I would have stayed for you.
If I had been braver,
I would have written myself a different ending.
But my love,
even as I go,
even as I step beyond the reach of your hands,
know this.
You were the only part of this world
that ever made me want to stay.
You will not see me again,
but if you stand in the wind long enough,
if you let the night settle around you,
if you listen in the hush between heartbeats,
you will know.
I never stopped loving you.
Not even now. Not even from the other side.

Forgive me.

And to my soul,
I am sorry.
I am sorry that I was never strong enough to hold you.
That I let the world make you small,
that I did not cradle you softly,
that I turned you away when you begged for warmth.
I am sorry that I forced you to wear this body,
to walk with a heart too heavy,
to breathe air that never felt like home.
I have let this world carve into you,
let it bruise and bend you,
let it strip you down to the marrow
until nothing was left but a whisper of what you were
meant to be.
I did not mean to abandon you.
I did not mean to leave you alone in the cold.
I just -
I just couldn't carry you any longer.
Perhaps in another life,
you will find someone who loves you better than I did.
Someone who lets you stay.
Someone who lets you bloom.

Forgive me.

I am unmaking myself.
I have carried this pain in my bones,
like stones grinding against each other,
like fractures that never healed,
like a weight pressing from the inside,
crushing me slow, silent,
inevitable.

The ghosts of my past do not whisper;
they scream.
They press their hands into my chest,
wrap their fingers around my ribs,
dragging me under, telling me it is time.
Even my cat watches the shadows gather,
ears twitching at the stillness that hangs in the air.
She sees it now.
She feels the air grow still.

I have tried.
God, I swear I have tried.

I have held on with hands that bled,
dragged myself through mornings that did not want me,
wrapped myself in voices that told me to stay,
but the voices fade, the light dims,
and I have no more words left to write.

I am unmaking myself.
Not dying;
erasing.

No footprints in the snow.
No echoes in the walls.
No name left behind.

Just silence.
Just stillness.
Just the quiet return
to the void that has always been waiting.

The sun will rise -
but I will not rise with it.
I was never here at all.

Forgive me,
for I do not deserve this gift.

I am undone. Completely. Finally.